SPEAK NOW
NEVER
HOLD YOUR PEACE
A MEMOIR

EBONI STIFF

Speak Now Never Hold Your Peace

The stories in the book reflect the author's recollection of events. Certain names, locations and identifying characteristics have been changed to protect the privacy of those depicted. The dialogues in the book have been re-created from the author's perspective and memory.

Copyright © 2023 by Eboni Stiff

All rights reserved. No part of this publication may be reproduced, distributed, or transmitted in any form or by any means, including photocopying, recording, scanning, or other electronic or mechanical methods, without the prior written permission of the publisher, except in the case of brief quotations embodied in critical reviews and certain other noncommercial uses permitted by copyright law. For permission requests, please contact ebonitheauthor@gmail.com

First Edition: January 2024

ISBN: 9798989376407 (paperback), 9798989376414 (ebook), 9798989376421 (paperback)

Library of Congress Control Number: 2023921765

Publisher: Eboni Mobley LLC

Printed in the United States

Edited By: Latrice Scott

Cover Photo By: Erick Robinson

Cover Photo Make-up Artist: Nachera "Cherry" Smith

***

To my wonderful Mother, my role model, my everything. Thank you for loving me unconditionally and I hope this book makes you proud.

In Loving Memory of my Father. There isn't a day that goes by that I don't miss you. Daddy, your baby girl is an author now. Keep watching over me. I love you beyond words.

In Loving Memory of my Sister. I love you so much and I wish you were here with me. I know you are smiling down on us all.

In Loving Memory of my Bonus Father. I miss our talks and your guidance. I pray that you are proud of mom and we love you forever.

Contents

Prologue	IX
Day 1: IT'S JUST GAS	1
Day 1 (Evening): FARTING IS IMPORTANT	9
DAY 2: QUESTIONS AND NO ANSWERS	15
DAY 3: CONFESSION OF THE DOCTOR	23
DAY 4: HAPPY BIRTHDAY MOMMY	27
DAY 5: THE VALLEY	31
DAY 6: EXPRESSIONS OF LOVE	37
DAY 7: ACCEPTANCE	41
DAY 8: SURVIVING THE NIGHT SHIFT	43
DAY 9: DEAR MOMMA	45
DAY 10: BRING ON THE TUBES	49
DAY 11: WHAT LAWSUIT?	53
DAY 12: SURPRISE	59
DAY 13: PARTY TIME	63
DAY 14: MOTHER/DAUGHTER BOND	69
DAY 15: SELF EDUCATION	73
DAY 16: LET IT OUT	75

DAY 17: TIME TO LIVE	81
Acknowledgements	84
About the Author	86

PROLOGUE

"We have to go now or she's going to die!", were the last words I heard from the doctor in the Emergency Room.

It was September 4, 2022 at approximately 3am that my life was getting ready to change forever. It felt as if the

anesthesia had already kicked in and I could barely keep my eyes open. I gave a thumbs up to my family and significant

other, Myles, as I was rolled down the hallway to the surgery room, not knowing if I would ever see them again.

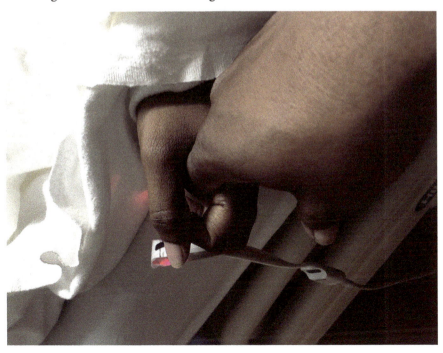

DAY 1: IT'S JUST GAS

Two days prior, I had a hysterectomy. The hysterectomy took place in the morning and I was sent home that evening. The doctor who performed the hysterectomy assured me that everything went well and cleared me to go home. I was told that it was important that I made a bowel movement or pass gas after this procedure.

A loud scream filled my bedroom in the middle of the night at approximately 10:00pm. Myles jumped from the bed, confused and continuously asking me what's wrong. I could barely speak. I was only able to let out loud moans and screams while holding my stomach. My stomach was cramping so bad and felt so tight that I could barely walk. I had never experienced pain like this in my life. Giving birth didn't hurt this bad. I slowly made my way to the bathroom hoping that I would be able to make a bowel movement or fart. Neither one of those things were happening. I sat on the toilet crying while rubbing my stomach and praying that I would make a bowel movement.

Myles was rubbing my back as I was sitting on the toilet and told me that I would feel better once I pooped. I was trying hard to poop, but it wasn't working.

About ten minutes had passed, but nothing happened and the pain intensified. I demanded to be taken to the hospital immediately. Myles said that he was going to call 911. I told him, absolutely not! I wanted to be taken to the hospital by car and to the hospital that performed the surgery. The ambulance would've taken me to the nearest hospital and that ride would have cost me a lot of money. Myles taking me to the hospital was free and I would be right back in the same place that operated on me two days ago. He asked if we should call the doctor and I said no. I just wanted to leave as soon as possible.

Myles went into the other room where my mother and aunt were sleeping. He advised them that I was in pain and that he was taking me back to the hospital. My mom and aunt came into my room and began asking me what's wrong and where were my clothes? Oh goodness, I didn't even realize I was naked. When they pointed that out, I really didn't care because I was in so much pain. I had no idea what happened to my pajamas! I went to bed with my clothes on and woke up without them. Too many things were happening in this moment and although clothes are important, it was the least of my worries.

I told Myles to get my blue maxi dress. After looking in both closets, he couldn't find it. As he continued looking for this blue dress, my mom started yelling at me and trying to convince me that it was just gas. She told me to lay back down and call the doctor. I asked her to stop yelling at me. She said she wasn't yelling, she just wanted me to calm down. She then turned to my aunt and told her to bring me some water. She said the water would make me feel better. Mom, I don't want any water. I needed pain medicine that was stronger than what I had! My aunt brought me a cup of water and it was cold. I tried to sip it and it seemed like my brain froze. I said oh no, this water is too cold. My mom told my aunt that the water should be hot. My aunt ran out of the room and came back with warm water. People, people, people, what are y'all doing? Can I please just go to the hospital? I don't want any cups of water.

Myles found a pink maxi dress and I went back into the bathroom to get dressed. When I looked in the bathroom mirror, I looked like I was ready to give birth to a baby. Why was my stomach so big and tight? Why was I in so much pain? This made absolutely no sense. I got dressed and I was ready to leave for the hospital.

My son, niece and Myles' son were asleep. We woke them up and advised them that I was going to the hospital because I was in pain, and we would all be back home soon.

Myles put me in the front seat of his car and my mom got into the back seat. We asked if my aunt was coming with us, and she said that she didn't know. As we started backing out of the driveway, my aunt came out of the house with a cup of coffee, ready to take the ride with us.

Finally, we were all in the car and ready for a 30-minute drive to the hospital. Myles asked me again if I wanted him to call 911 and I refused. As we were driving, his car was hitting every single bump along the way, intensifying my pain. I told Myles to please stop hitting every single bump in the road! He said it wasn't his fault our roads are raggedly and it's dark outside. I was extremely annoyed, but I needed to make it to the hospital, and he was the driver. I just closed my eyes, pretending to be asleep. Myles didn't know where the hospital was located because he does not live in this city. My aunt was giving Myles directions to the hospital from the GPS on her phone. As we were riding along the interstate, there were signs that it was closed in a few miles because of an accident. I was asked to lead the way from that point. I knew the GPS would re-route but I didn't have the energy to explain that. Somehow, I was able to muster up the strength and advise him on how to get to the hospital. As we approached the main entrance, my mom yelled out from the back seat, this hospital is closed. Mom, what hospital is closed? My aunt agreed with her and said it sure does look closed. I could only laugh to myself inside. The pain was too great to laugh out loud.

Myles ran inside and asked if he was in the right area because he didn't see any emergency room signs. Suddenly, a man appeared at the car with a wheelchair. I was immediately rolled into the hospital and down the hallway to the ER reception area. After approximately twenty minutes, I was taken to a room for further evaluation.

They started an IV and gave me pain medicine. Life began to look better at this point because my pain was almost non-existent. I thought I would be going home soon because they were able to take my pain away with the medicine administered. I felt like my pain was under control and there really wasn't a reason to stay. I was able to mentally function and thank Myles for getting me to the hospital safely.

The nurse advised me that I would be going to the back for a series of scans and tests so they could determine why I was having so much pain. After several tests, the nurse came into the room and the tone changed. The energy felt different, and I knew something was wrong. The nurse assigned to my room began telling me that I couldn't eat or drink anything for the rest of the evening. I asked why? Because those orders didn't make sense. I asked if I could have water and she said no. She offered no explanation and said that I had to wait for the doctor to come in.

While I was waiting on the doctor, my mother, aunt, and Myles alternated coming into the room to spend time with me. The hospital still had COVID regulations in place, so I could only have one person in the room at a time. Myles was in the room with me for a while as I was going in and out of sleep. He went to the waiting room to tell my mother to come in, but her and my aunt were sleeping back to back. He came back into the room to tell me; I laughed and said, it's okay, don't wake them up. I knew I should be going home in a little while because I feel better. I really just wanted to fart or make a bowel movement so I could go home. I felt like this was the only thing keeping me there.

Myles and I began reflecting on the moments in our bedroom right before we left for the hospital. We laughed about my aunt bringing me warm water and everyone just being confused in the moment. I was happy that my aunt was here with us. She is the support we all needed, especially my mom. My aunt is my mother's childhood best friend. They are truly sisters and I love being around them.

The ER doctor came into the room while Myles and I were talking. The doctor believed that there was something wrong with my intestines and that I would require surgery to repair the damage. My intestines? How did something happen to my intestines? He wasn't quite sure yet, but he ordered more testing to do a further evaluation. After he received the results from those tests, he advised that he would return to the room and discuss a more detailed treatment plan with us. The doctor explained that I was going to need surgery, but the results from the new tests would determine the details of that surgery.

Myles left the room to give my mother and aunt the news. My mother came into the room and she apologized for not listening to me while we were at the house. She applauded me for listening to my body and coming back to the hospital. There was no way she could have known that it was this serious. I wasn't mad at my mother and I told her that there was no need to apologize.

Afterwards, my aunt came into the room. I said to her, I told you I didn't need any water. She laughed and it made me feel so good. My aunt's laughter can light up any room and make you feel good, no matter what you are going through. After spending a few more moments together, she decided to leave the room to check on my mother. That was the best thing to do because my mother is very sensitive. I wanted my mother to know that I was going to be fine and her best friend was the right person to tell her that.

The doctor came back into the room but this time it was with a sense of urgency in his voice. The doctor advised me that my body was septic and I would need to have surgery ASAP. This would be considered an emergency surgery. He stated this was very serious and normally the hospital doesn't open up the OR (operating room) on a Sunday, but this needed to be done. Not really knowing the severity of what he was saying, I said okay without asking any questions and he left the room.

I didn't really understand what it meant for your body to be septic. I could only think of a septic tank and I knew that held waste. If that is what my body was equivalent to, I was in trouble.

The nurse came into the room and I signed a series of authorization papers.

I don't know how much time had passed from the time I initially arrived, but it had to be at least a few hours because my pain level was starting to rise again. The nurse wouldn't allow me to drink anything in preparation for surgery. The only way I could get water was to take medicine by mouth, so I chose that option. The nurse gave me the pills and I took them one by one just so I could have water. The nurse left the room and there was a cup of water on the counter. I asked Myles to sneak me some water and he did. That's what I'm talking about. Give me some water! The nurse came back into the room and stated that she needed a urine sample from me to make sure I wasn't pregnant before the surgery. I refused to get up and use the bathroom because my pain level was back up to at least eight. The nurse became very upset with me because I repeatedly refused her request to give a urine sample for a pregnancy test. If I were not in so much pain, I would have done it. The nurse was upset with me and I was upset with her. I told her this hospital has my reproductive organs, it wasn't possible for me to be pregnant and I'm not getting up to give a urine sample. After I kept refusing, the doctor told her I was correct, and the sample wasn't necessary. He said if he needed anything he could get it while I was in the operating room.

More time passed and the doctor came back into the room with more news. I was told that in addition to the surgery, I would definitely need a colostomy bag. I only knew what colostomy bags were from the television. I didn't know of anyone who had a colostomy bag. I asked the doctor if he was sure and he said yes. He told me that he was 100% positive that I would wake up with a colostomy bag. My body was so septic that it was killing me and this was the only way to save my life. I agreed to the surgery, signed the papers and waited to be taken back to the OR.

Myles did not like what he heard and repeatedly asked me if I understood. Yes, I understand. Bag or Die. Ummm....Bag me please!

While I waited to be taken to the operating room for the procedure, the nurses gave me antibiotics and told me they were putting medicine through my IV to make me relax. As the medicine began to take effect, I told Myles that I was wondering if I would see my father in the operating room. I think that may have scared him because my father is deceased. The last time I saw my father was while I was under anesthesia for a previous operation years ago. Myles was speechless and I drifted off to sleep. While I was asleep, Myles held my hand and said a prayer. The nurses allowed everyone in the room to see me right before the surgery and that made me afraid. I was thinking, I must be on my way to Heaven because why are they letting everyone in here at the same time to see me now? What happened to the COVID protocol?

I could see the pain in my mother's eyes and it hurt so bad. Who wants to hear that their child could possibly die, three days before their birthday? Nobody. My mother was standing there looking at her only living child, fight another fight. She was the one who said it was gas and suggested that I lay back down until tomorrow. Had I laid back down, tomorrow would have never arrived for me. I know she was carrying that guilt with her in that moment. It wasn't her fault. I love her so much and I know she would never purposely give me advice to hurt me. My mom kissed me on my forehead and left the room. She told Myles to stand in the gap because she just wasn't strong enough. I understood and respected her decision.

My aunt told me that she prayed and I was going to be okay. She said that no weapon formed against me shall prosper.

Myles said again, do you understand? I assured him that I understood what needed to be done. Myles had more questions because he thought I was high off drugs, which he was probably right. Myles wanted a second opinion, but I wasn't that high. I knew we didn't have time for that. The more questions Myles asked, the more I believed the doctor wanted to leave. The doctor knew that this was scary for him so he assured Myles that he would do the best he could and that I was top priority. Finally, the doctor told Myles, "We have to go now or she's going to die".

Okay Myles, we can talk later. He held my hand, took another picture, and kissed me on my forehead. I gave him another thumbs up as I was rolled down the hallway. As soon as the hospital bed turned the corner, I was asleep.

DAY 1 (EVENING): FARTING IS IMPORTANT

I am high as a kite laying in this hospital bed. As I was laying on my back in the hospital bed, my phone made a noise indicating that I received a text message. It was my son. He was planning a sleepover with his friends in the neighborhood. I advised him that the sleepover was fine as long as the other parents agreed. I did not want him to know exactly what was going on. I wanted him to be a kid and enjoy the Labor Day weekend.

I am thankful these hospital rooms are private because I didn't want a stranger seeing me like this. I didn't even want to see me like this. NG-tube in my nose, another tube in my neck, drainage tube in my stomach and a colostomy bag. What is really going on here is all I am thinking? The pain medicine I was given gave me a euphoric feeling and that helped with the mental anguish I was experiencing. The room was empty. Where was my mom, aunt and Myles? How long was my surgery? Why am I alone? I remember a nurse coming in to wake me up. I asked if I was in recovery and she said no. I was in my assigned room on the third floor of the hospital. It was Sunday evening and because the OR was technically closed, they brought me up to my room, instead of going to the recovery area. I asked the nurse where my family was and she didn't know. The anesthesia was wearing off and it was causing me to be in and out of sleep. The nurses were extremely nice and constantly evaluated my pain level. I felt no pain during that time. Each time I woke up, I wanted to know where my family was.

When I woke up the third time, Myles was there. He was telling me how proud everyone was of me and how good I was doing. They were all so proud of me, but honestly, I was proud of them. Last night was insane, but by the grace of God, we managed to pull it together and save my life. That was something to be proud of.

Myles was standing to my right and I tried to roll over on my right side while we were talking and I quickly turned on my back because it hurt. I forgot I had a colostomy bag attached to the right side of my stomach. I could only lay on my back or the left side at the moment. I asked Myles to stand on my left side and he didn't have a problem with my request.

I told Myles that I didn't get to see my daddy this time while I was in surgery. Myles was speechless. I guess that comment was awkward but I needed to say it. I mean, there really was nothing to say in reference to that comment, but I felt that it was important for me to say that. Myles told me that he took my mom and aunt home after they saw me and got the report from the doctor. I felt so bad because I don't remember seeing anyone the first time I woke up from surgery. Myles showed me pictures and videos of me waking up from the operation the first time. Those videos were hilarious. I was making funny noises, licking my tongue out at them and trying to dance.

Apparently, the ostomy care team also came and gave directions while I was still heavily medicated from the surgery. I was told that my mother understood all of the information given by the ostomy care team. I never understood that. Why give someone instructions when they are clearly high on medication? It makes no sense.

The doctor advised them that I needed to rest so they went home and Myles came back to spend the night with me.

The nurse came in and gave me a series of antibiotics and other medication through the IV. The nurse told me that I could administer myself pain medicine through the PCA by pushing a button that was in the bed with me. She said the pain medicine was on a timer, so even if I pushed it three times in five minutes, it would only administer what it is supposed to. That was good to know because it prevents possible overdose and many other problems that could occur with someone giving themselves pain medicine. I have a high tolerance for pain, so I didn't anticipate that I would be pushing the button often. The nurse also told me where the buttons were to call for help and how to control the television.

I was given instructions to call for help each time I needed to use the bathroom because I was hooked up to machines for the IV and I was a fall risk patient. I understood everything the nurse told me and she left the room.

As I was laying in the bed, the blankets and hospital gown were covering the colostomy bag. I wasn't ready to look at it, so I didn't. I pretended like it wasn't there because this could not be my life right now. I did not want to see the colostomy bag. I was not ready to accept it. I was devastated.

Myles asked, do you remember what happened last night and earlier today? I said yes. He told me that I was being mean in the car ride over to the hospital because he could not control the bumps and I was yelling at him. I laughed first and apologized second. I explained to him that I wasn't being mean, I was in pain. There's a big difference. He started imitating my voice and re-enacting what happened in the car. I think Myles is a comedian and I was thankful for his efforts to make me laugh and smile. I laughed and told him I do not sound like a baby. I was happy that we were able to laugh at this moment because my life was in danger and we had no idea.

I find that to be a very serious problem for many patients. We rely on the doctor and the entire time, we should be relying on what our body is telling us, what God is telling us. If something doesn't feel right, it's not right. Demand the help you deserve.

As we laughed, it got serious, very quickly. I had to hear what the doctor told him, my mother and my aunt while I was in recovery.

He described being told what happened to me like being in a movie. He said they were called into some area of the hospital that he didn't know existed. After entering through the doors of this area, he noticed a big table and a few chairs. After they sat down, the doctor immediately said she is going to be fine and that eased some of their anxiety.

The doctor proceeded to tell my family that during my hysterectomy, the doctor who performed that surgery made a mistake and punctured my colon during the operation. My eyes got so big and tears formed as I was listening to him. I asked multiple times if he was sure that is what the doctor told him. Myles said that the doctor who made the mistake called and told him what she had done to me. After puncturing my colon, I was sent home without being told that it was punctured and basically left to die. The puncture allowed the food to escape the intestines and everything I ate for the past two days was floating around in my body, poisoning my system. The doctor was surprised that I did not have a fever when I came into the emergency room. The doctor said if I hadn't come in last night, I would not have survived through the night. I began crying as Myles was talking to me and describing what the doctor was telling them. Myles stopped and said, "Oh no, we are strong, there will be no crying."

I think that is a man thing because I needed to let it out. I had to cry. There were so many things going through my head. I was crying because I was angry, grateful, sad, happy, confused and mad; all at the same time.

After a few minutes, I was able to stop crying and Myles continued telling me what was said during their meeting with the doctor. The doctor told him that the plan was for me to stay in the hospital for a few days, learn about the colostomy bag and then I should be able to go home once my bowels were functioning.

The doctor assured my family that he cleaned my body extremely well and even joked about finding collard greens in my system. My auntie cooked those collard greens and they were good when I ate them!

The doctor repaired my colon by closing the hole created from the puncture with stitches. The purpose of the colostomy bag was to give my colon time to heal from the surgery. My stool would be released in the bag directly from my intestines, which would allow my colon to rest and heal properly. Once the colon was healed, I would be able to have the colostomy bag reversed. If everything went as the doctor's expected them to, he predicted that I would only have to wear the colostomy bag for a minimum of four months.

I asked Myles again if he was one thousand percent sure that the doctor said my colon was punctured during the hysterectomy. He said yes. I wished I hadn't asked him that because I got very angry.

What type of doctor punctures their patient's colon and sends them home? I started thinking about all the things I hear about black people, especially women, and hospitals. Was I on my way to becoming a statistic? After all, she did tell me to wait until Monday to come back if I was still in pain. If I would've listened to her and not myself, I would not be alive. I made a choice to choose myself every single time. If something doesn't feel right, I am going to get help and I am going to advocate for myself. I was in shock, confused, disappointed in my previous doctor, mad, grateful to be alive and happy all at the same time. How is that even possible? How do I unpack all these emotions and still smile, knowing that I was one fart away from life or death? God is the only answer to that question.

DAY 2: QUESTIONS AND NO ANSWERS

It's Labor Day, so I assume the doctors were not working today. The doctor's team came in my room around 6am. The team appeared to be very nice as they asked me a series of questions. They wanted to know how I slept, what was my pain level, and they told me they wanted me to try to get out of bed and walk. I slept well because of the anesthesia and medication. My pain level was a 4 and I agreed to sit in the chair as long as I could. The tech placed a few blankets and a "donut" in the chair to make it comfortable for me.

The nurses also advised me that the plan was to take the tube out of my nose and neck within the next few days. Once those tubes were removed, I would be placed on a clear liquid diet. I was excited about that. Although I was excited, I was scared to eat. What if there was still a small hole and more food leaked out? Would I be septic again? Mentally, I was really messed up. I didn't know what to do or how to feel.

Myles left the room to go eat breakfast and I was left alone with my thoughts.

I had conflicting feelings about being in this hospital. On one hand my life was saved and on the other hand, my life was almost taken away from the same hospital. I had to figure out how to separate the overall hospital, from one doctor who happens to work at the hospital. I told myself that I shouldn't blame the entire hospital for the mistake of this one doctor. It was a difficult task, but I was up for the challenge.

When Myles came back into the hospital room from breakfast, I was sitting in the chair. He was so happy that he sat on my hospital bed and made a video. That was fun. I pretended to be super strong and put both of my hands in the air, flexing my pretend arm muscles. I had no muscles but I enjoyed making those videos. I asked Myles to help me to the bathroom so I could brush my teeth. He unplugged the IV machine so I could walk to the bathroom, and I was able to brush my teeth. That felt really good because my mouth had a stale taste, and I just knew my breath was stank.

Myles asked me a lot of questions about how I was feeling and if I knew anything about the colostomy bag. I told him that I did not know much. I didn't want to know. In some weird way, I convinced myself that if I didn't talk about it, it wasn't real. Myles respected my decision, and we did not discuss the bag.

The nurses came into the room to check on me and they were so excited that I was still sitting in the chair. All I really wanted to do was lay down. I don't like to push myself too soon or too hard because as my late grandmother would say, "you're going to have a setback". I just wanted to leave the hospital as soon as possible. Therefore, if sitting in the chair would get me home, let's do it.

As time passed, Myles had to prepare to leave. Myles had to return to work in his city, hundreds of miles away. I was extremely sad. I didn't want to see him go, but nobody planned for this to happen. Life must go on is what I told myself to make me feel better. That didn't work.

Myles wanted to see the colostomy bag before he left. Truth is, I wasn't ready to look at it because that made my situation real. Here goes, time to see it. I felt ugly and disfigured. I thought my stomach looked a mess, there is a scar down the middle of it and my belly button is consumed inside of the scar. Please, just put the gown back down. Let me be. He assured me that I was beautiful and kissed me on the forehead. It felt good to be loved despite a poop bag hanging from my body. He gave me a hug and a kiss on the lips. Just like that, I was alone in my room.

I was able to get some sleep before my mom and auntie arrived. My mom was there to check on my well-being and get some answers from the doctor who caused this mayhem. The doctor who punctured my colon was off work for the day and I was happy about that. I really didn't feel like seeing her. It was too soon.

A woman came into my room with lots of stuff in her hand. She was smiling and had a very positive attitude. She announced that she was from the ostomy care team. She was there to check the colostomy bag and give me literature to read. I asked her to lay the paperwork on the other side of the room and I would get to it when I was feeling up to it. The colostomy bag had stool in it and she emptied it while I laid in the bed. During this time, I just closed my eyes and asked the Lord for strength to deal with this situation.

The nurses changed shifts every day around 6:30 pm. Each time the shift changes, the person taking over comes in, introduces themselves, reviews my medications and any activity I had prior to them starting their shirt.

The nurses said they had good news. They received orders to remove the NG-tube from my nose and the other tube from my neck. I never got the name of the tube that was placed in my neck. I didn't care what the name of the tube was, I was grateful that it was being removed. We were all excited because those were two less tubes coming from my body. My mom recorded the NG tube being removed from my nose. The tube is extremely long, and the removal process hurt. As the nurse was gently pulling the tube out, the nurse and my mom kept telling me to breathe and encouraging me by saying you are doing good. My mom and aunt were my biggest cheerleaders and it felt great having them by my side.

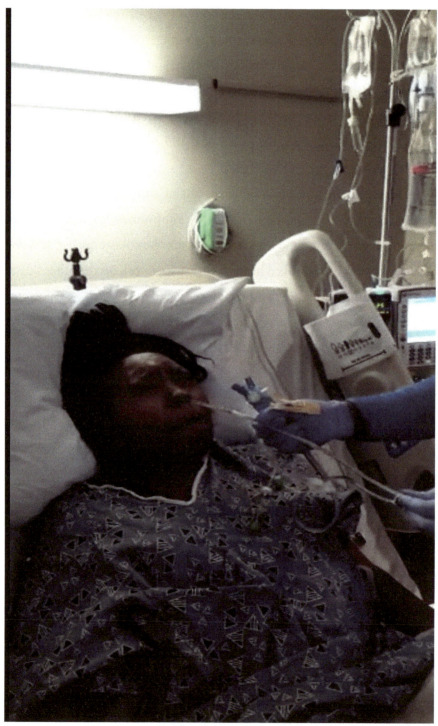
NG Tube being removed.

The tube being removed from my neck didn't hurt at all. I was relieved and free from tubes.

The nurse examined my stomach, said it was still swollen, and I was given Gas-X.

I sat in the chair for at least another hour. Although I feel like I made good progress, I really just want to lay down and sleep. Going from the chair to the bed caused me to have shortness of breath. I stayed up because my mom and aunt were in the room with me. I wanted to show them how strong I was. Being strong for others can sometimes hurt.

Another professional came in and advised me of what foods I could and couldn't eat with the colostomy bag. Say what now? I know nothing about this bag, barely want to look at it, and now my diet has completely changed? I felt like I was being repeatedly kicked while I was down. For every good thing that happened, bad news was given. What is really going on with my life? Popcorn, certain fruits, peanuts, or salads just to name a few, were the foods that were on the NON-APPROVED list. What's ironic is, the moment someone tells you that you can't have something, is literally the moment you want it. I didn't understand why there was such a list.

The professional explained that I must stay away from food that could potentially clog my stoma. The stoma has a small hole that releases stool from my intestines. If I ate food on the non-approved list, my stoma could potentially get clogged, there would be no output and worst-case scenario, I would need surgery to correct it. I was grateful for this information because I did not want to do anything that was going to require me to have another surgery. This information was a lot to take in for one person. Do this, don't do that, eat this, don't eat that. It became very overwhelming. My diet was officially clear liquids. The more I thought about it, the more I became upset. I didn't remain upset very long because I have faith in God. I believed that this was all happening to me for a greater purpose.

My mother kept herself busy contacting our family, friends and my co-workers. I had to give her the password to my phone to reach certain individuals. We watched television until I fell asleep. As my mom and aunt prepared to leave, I asked her to put the phone on the other side of the room because I was just too tired to talk to anyone. Before going to sleep, I had to make arrangements with my mother, aunt and niece to get my son to and from school while I was hospitalized.

Prior to this incident, I drove my son to school, picked him up and took him to track practice after school three days a week. My mother and I wanted to keep my son on his daily routine as much as possible in efforts to minimize his emotional trauma. Before they left the hospital, we had a good plan for my son. My mother and aunt were going to alternate taking him to and from school. They were going to try their best to get him to every track practice; but couldn't make any guarantees. I was satisfied knowing that my son was going to have a consistent ride to and from school. We were under the assumption that this plan was supposed to last for just a few days.

We were wrong.

DAY 3: CONFESSION OF THE DOCTOR

Word was spreading fast throughout my family, friends and co-workers about what happened to me. My good friend who used to work at this hospital came to visit me. We were in the room making a video and in walks the doctor who performed the hysterectomy and made a mistake during my surgery. The room got extremely quiet and the feeling of anger took over me. She proceeds to explain why I was in the hospital and the treatment plan. At this moment, she doesn't know how long I am going to have the colostomy bag or how long I am going to be in the hospital because my bowels aren't "waking" up. What does that mean? My bowels aren't waking up? I didn't ask her because I really didn't want to speak to her at this point. The colostomy bag had stool in it, so I really didn't understand what she meant when she said that my bowels weren't waking up. I just wanted her to leave as soon as possible. As a patient, I would've been okay with her owning up to her mistake at the time of the hysterectomy, keeping me for at least one day for evaluation and then sending me home. In my opinion, that would have been the appropriate thing to do. Did the doctor do that? Absolutely not. She sent me home the same day of my hysterectomy, knowing that she punctured my colon. To make matters worst, she didn't say a word and didn't put it in my chart. Here she was standing there apologizing. I couldn't believe this woman was standing in front of me saying she's sorry that she failed and promised to be more careful with other patients. She said I may not believe it, but this has never happened before. No, I don't believe this has never happened before.

While I was home for two days following the hysterectomy, I did not make a bowel movement and I did not pass gas. I continuously called the hospital to tell the nurses that I was in pain. The nurses felt it was unusual and told me that I should not be in this much pain. I agreed but it did not take away the fact that I was in pain and nobody had answered. You would think that the nurses would've told me that my colon was punctured and I needed to come back to the hospital. The nurses never gave me that information. You know why they weren't able to give me this information? The doctor failed to put it in my chart. She willfully and purposely left this very important information out of my files. Even after I complained via the telephone, she told the nurses to advise me that if I wasn't feeling better by Monday, to come back into the office. Well, it's a great thing I didn't follow her advice! I would've been dead on Sunday and a dead body would've been rolling into a morgue on Monday. Listening to my body, advocating for myself and going right back to the hospital on Saturday night and not Monday as she suggested saved my life. Not passing a bowel movement and not being able to fart was a clear sign to me that something was wrong. I didn't care what anyone said, I had to advocate for myself to save myself. The doctor's apology did not feel genuine because I felt like she was only apologizing because she got caught. Apologizing after the discovery of something you tried to cover up isn't really an I'm sorry for what I did, it's more like, I'm sorry I got caught.

I looked to my friend and she gave me the signal to just remain quiet. My facial expressions told her that I was angry. The doctor asked me if I had questions and I said no. She left the room with her team and I was extremely upset. My friend held up her phone and told me she had the entire confession and apology on video. Now that's a great friend. If you don't have one like her, I don't know what to tell you. She sat with me for hours and made sure I had Gatorade and food from the approved list. I was so appreciative that she took time out of her day to spend with me.

The nurses came in shortly after my friend left and took me for a walk outside of the room. I walked maybe ten steps before asking to turn around. I was experiencing shortness of breath and just wanted to lay down. The nurse allowed me to lay down and get some rest.

My stomach was hurting and I was feeling nauseous. The pain medicine helped for only a few hours and I was given Zofran for nausea. That made me feel better temporarily. Overall, I just didn't feel good.

My mom came later that night. I told her what happened with the doctor and played the video for her. She was very upset and assured me that I would be back to normal in due time. She stayed the night with me, and my aunt stayed home with my son. We didn't get a lot of rest because the machines kept beeping and the night crew was the worst. They took over twenty minutes to respond to requests and at some point my mother said don't call them anymore, I will take care of you. That made me feel worse. Not only has her life altered just to help me, now she has to be the night nurse? Lord, get me out of here!

DAY 4: HAPPY BIRTHDAY MOMMY

Happy Birthday Mom! She is the best mother in the world. She spent the morning of her birthday in the hospital with me and I had conflicting emotions about it. Yes, I was glad to be alive and celebrating with her, but of course the hospital was not the ideal place for her to be. Just for my mom, I pushed myself to take laps around the nurses' desk. My mother was so happy. She recorded me and hearing the excitement in her voice let me know that I was doing the right thing. Walking around the nurses' station and smiling was the only gift I could give to my mother for her birthday. I apologized and she told me to stop. She was happy that I was alive and that was good enough for her.

My aunt arrived at the hospital, and she began to tell us how she got lost taking my son to school. It was the funniest thing I had heard all morning. She got on the interstate in the wrong direction and my son didn't say anything to her, he just fell asleep. I checked my cell phone, and he texted me, we are lost with a crying face emoji. I asked my aunt how was she able to figure out how to get him to school? She never did. She took him back home and my niece, Ash, took him to school. We laughed for such a long time about this incident.

Someone from the ostomy care wound team came into my room with a kit. It was time to change the bag. I laid there with my eyes closed as she explained how to change the bag. I still wasn't ready to accept that this was a part of my life. My mother took pictures and notes on how to change it. Although my eyes were closed, I heard every word she said. Despite my unwillingness to open my eyes, the woman was nice and I appreciated her for being there.

It was early in the afternoon, and I convinced my mom and aunt to leave so they could celebrate my mother's birthday.

The daytime nurses and techs were extremely supportive, helped me to the bathroom,

and offered encouraging words each time they came into my room. The only reason I needed help from them to go to the bathroom was because I was hooked up to the IV machines. The IV was giving me fluids and pain medicine. Once the machines weren't connected to the wall, I was able to use the walker in my room to go to the bathroom.

As I was watching TV, there was a knock at the door. Only doctors and nurses knock, so who could this be? It was a woman there to give me a massage! We get massages in the hospital? Oh yes, I was so excited. I didn't know this service existed for patients. Let me tell you, she could come to my room anytime of the day or night. As a matter of fact, just don't leave the room. The massage eased my state of mind. It made me forget where I was and why I was there. It was the best mental medicine that I received since I was there. After that massage, it was lights out for me until shift change.

It was time for the night shift. The nurses were nice. It was the techs that were assigned to my room that never wanted to work. One of their tasks was to unhook the machines so I could go to the bathroom. Their response time was almost 30-45 minutes and it seemed like an eternity. Their fix to what they viewed as a problem was to hook me up to something that suctioned urine. It looked like a banana, sits between your legs, and as you urinate, it suctions it. It's similar to a Pure Wick. This has got to be the laziest thing to give a patient that is capable of walking. I felt so conflicted.

The doctors wanted me up and walking more to "wake" up my bowels, but because it was an inconvenience to the night techs, I was forced to lay in bed and urinate into some banana looking thing. The night was extremely rough. I waited 45 minutes to be changed from that stupid pee thing they placed between my legs. When the suction doesn't work, the urine just sits on me. I'm already not allowed to bathe and now I have urine soaking on me for 45 minutes. The worst part is, each time I had to be changed, it required me to sit up in the chair so the sheets could be changed as well. Ultimately, I was getting less sleep. Due to the fact that I wasn't getting much rest throughout the night, I was tired during the day.

DAY 5: THE VALLEY

The doctors came in again at 6am and ordered another CT scan. I told them that I was feeling nauseous and had pain in my stomach. As for liquids, I was tolerating small sips of Gatorade.

The purpose of the CT scan was to see how well my body was recovering from the second surgery and to measure my bowel movement. The CT scan revealed no bowel movement through my intestines and that was not a good sign. From what I understood, the surgery was supposed to correct my punctured colon and the colostomy bag was in place to give my colon time to heal. Unfortunately, nothing was going as the doctors planned. I was so frustrated and confused.

My body experienced two traumatic events within three days of each other and they were surprised my bowels weren't waking up? I was not surprised. At this point, I don't even know if the hysterectomy surgery was a success because we are dealing with a different crisis; my colon being punctured. So, what does my bowels not waking up mean for me and my treatment plan? It means that the NG-tube must be placed back through my nose and down my throat to my stomach.

My mother arrived at the hospital, and I gave her the update in reference to the tube being placed back in. We prayed with each other, and afterwards, all I could do was cry. The first time the tube was put in, I was asleep in surgery. Therefore, I didn't feel them inserting the tube. This time, I was going to be awake and did not know what to expect. It was the unknown that made me nervous. The nurse prepared me as much as she could physically, however it was my mental that needed to be prepared. As the nurse put this long tube back through my nose, I was given instructions to breathe. I squeezed my mother's hand tightly as tears rolled down my face. The tube is placed back in and there is tape on my nose to hold it in place.

As soon as the tube was put in, green bile filled a bucket that was on the wall behind the bed. The bile filled the bucket so quickly that the nurse had to call for help. The nurse was very cautious with the bucket because she said the bile could burn you if it touches the skin. The bile in this bucket was a clear indicator that my bowels were still asleep. A patient is limited to how long they can remain in the condition that I was in. There was no bowel activity and bile was filling the buckets quickly. The doctors were growing concerned and trying to think of another plan if my bowels did not begin functioning soon.

DAY 5: THE VALLEY

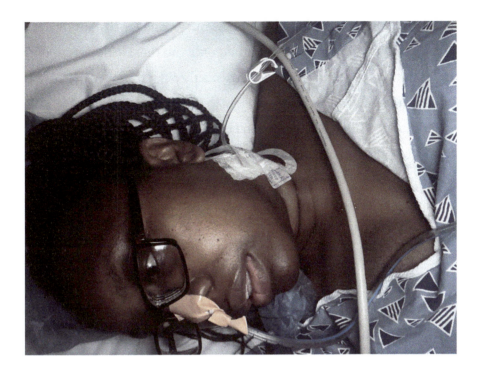

After my bile output slowed down, the nurses told me that my diet was restricted to no foods or liquids. I could only rub those little wet sponges across my lips. I had to receive all nutrients through the IV. My heart was broken in less than ten minutes.

My mom and aunt left the hospital because it was time to pick up Marc from school. I told them not to come back because I was honestly starting to feel depressed. I did not want this tube back down my throat, and I couldn't eat or drink anything? Life was not looking too great.

Myles was back in South Florida and overly concerned because he had been texting me for two days and hadn't received a response. I wasn't trying to ignore him or anyone else for that matter. I was just trying to feel better.

Later in the afternoon, I was able to text him back. I told him the "CAT scan showed no bowel movement, tube back in, fighting for my life". He replied, "we better fight".

I was thinking about praying. It was just me and God this afternoon. I silenced my phone, turned off the television, and had a conversation with God. I understood that this was my valley and that I wasn't alone, although I felt alone. I told God that I know this isn't my ending but asked what was it a beginning to? I prayed for Him to help me understand all of this, dry the tears from my eyes, clear the confusion from my mind, and lift my spirits when I am down. I prayed for strength, but I honestly didn't want to be strong anymore. I wanted to be weak. I wanted to let the world know that I wasn't feeling okay. I wanted to scream. I wanted to rip the bag from my side and be normal. Nobody understood but God. Whenever someone asks, how are you? I feel programmed to say, I am okay. I really wasn't okay. I needed a therapist. I asked for one, but not one human showed up. It was in this moment that I realized God was my therapist and it was my job to cast my cares upon Him. I will be okay in due time. People always say, God gives the strongest battles to the toughest soldiers. I was thinking, God how strong am I supposed to be? This is strong, but on steroids. I wanted God to take me off the strong soldiers list as soon as possible. I told Him that too. If you can't have a real conversation with God, then something is wrong. He spoke back and told me, He isn't finished with me yet and prepare to continue to be strong.

It was late and I got a knock at the door. Myles walked in with a beautiful purple flower and a smile. He told me that he had to see me because he was concerned. He said when he left a few days ago, I was doing fine. Then to receive a text message two days later that I was fighting for my life didn't make sense. He was there to make sure I wasn't giving up and to give me comfort.

DAY 6: EXPRESSIONS OF LOVE

I am musty. I smell myself and it isn't good at all. I haven't had a bath in eight days. Although I wasn't approved to take a bath, I was approved to use the bath wipes to clean myself. I commend the nurses because I know my room must've smelled bad when they came to check on me. However, they never complained. Maybe my nurses are used to funky smells. Either way, I absolutely loved every nurse that entered my room and I definitely didn't want to smell bad.

Myles wiped me off with the bath wipes and told a lot of jokes to brighten up my day. After making sure I was clean, he left to get some food.

It was a good thing that I cleaned myself with bath wipes because my cousin came to visit me today. She was concerned because I hadn't answered my phone in two days. I absolutely love her to pieces. She was there to make sure I was doing well. She is one person I could be honest with and say that I was not in a good place mentally. My cousin assured me that she would do anything in her power to help me get to a place where I could feel good about myself again. She volunteered to help get Marc to school and to bring food to the house if my mom or aunt didn't feel like cooking. I was thankful for the time she spent with me today.

Myles, my mom, and aunt came back into the room together. My mom told me that my family, friends, and co-workers were concerned because I wasn't responding to any text messages or phone calls. I just wasn't in the mood, especially yesterday. It was my time in the "valley" with God. I promised her that I would read my messages and respond to everyone who took the time to contact me.

It was Friday and I didn't want her spending the weekend here. Myles was there and I told her to go home to get a break.

I spent part of the evening responding to text messages. There were over 100 messages! I didn't know people cared so much about me and I was grateful for it. There were a lot of prayers, positivity, uplifting quotes, bible scriptures and pictures of old times with me and my friends.

I had a few real estate deals that were falling apart because my clients were not able to get in contact with me. I reached out to them via text and explained to them what was happening. They were very sympathetic and offered support. I was coming to the realization that my career and the ability to provide for my family was being negatively impacted because of the carelessness of one person. I was able to text my boss and my lender in reference to deals I had on the verge of closing. My lender and boss assured me that they would handle my deals. Many of my colleagues offered their help and sent flowers and fruit baskets to my hospital room.

The texts that touched me the most were the text messages from Marc, Bri and Ash. Marc was simply missing his mother. I called Marc and he wanted to know when I was coming home. I had no answer to give Marc and it broke my heart. As a mother, if you don't have the answer, who does? I assured him that I would continue to fight to make it home to him as soon as I could. We agreed that he could visit me next week. We told each other "I love you" and I had to hang up the phone so he wouldn't hear me cry. I missed him so much. I took my son to school every morning, picked him up, took him to track practice, and had nightly talks before bed each night in our home. I was no longer able to do any of those things from this hospital bed. Nonetheless, it gave me the strength to keep going so I could make it home to my son.

Bri is my oldest daughter. She just started her college journey in South Florida. I didn't want her to worry about me, so I sent her a text that I was okay and promised I would be home soon. At the moment, the text worked and I was satisfied with that. How do I know it worked? She asked me to send her some money. She was my broke best friend at the time. I sent her the funds through an app and she was happy. As a mother, her being able to focus on school and complete college was more important than what I was going through. Mommy would be fine.

My niece Ash is living with me after experiencing the loss of her beautiful mother, my sister Tasha. My sister lost her battle with breast cancer a few years ago. I could never replace my sister and I hope that I am making her proud with my niece. My niece wanted to know when I was coming home and when she could come visit. That made me feel so special because she is young, working, and stepped in to help with Marc in such a big way. She started helping take him to school in the mornings, pick him up, and take him to track practice. What would I have done without her helping me? I really don't know. My niece and my mother came up with a plan that would help the household. My niece quit her job at the daycare so that she could be in a better position to help take her little cousin to and from school. My mother (her grandmother) paid her weekly and it all worked out. Everyone was sacrificing because of me, and I was truly grateful.

After responding to text messages, I asked Myles to put my phone away. I really wasn't feeling the best and it was because I was mentally drained. There were so many thoughts going through my mind and I just wanted it all to stop. I didn't talk to Myles much because it hurt so bad with the tube in my throat. We took pictures together so that we could look back on this moment and give hope to someone else who may be experiencing something similar. Myles held my hand, and I asked him to pray. I love to hear him pray! He was doing everything in his power to make me feel better and it was working. He started watching television and I went to sleep.

DAY 7: ACCEPTANCE

Myles left early this morning and my aunt went back home with him.

I was very drowsy today from the medication and all I wanted to do was sleep. I think it had something to do with Myles and my aunt leaving. Selfishly I wanted both of them to stay.

The colostomy bag had small amounts of stool and started leaking. Someone from the ostomy care team came in and changed it. Today I was a big girl and decided to watch the nurse change the bag. I took a few mental notes. I was slowly coming to terms with the fact that this will be my new life. She put on a two-piece bag. One piece is circular and sticks to my skin, I refer to it as a base. The base has clamps so the second piece can be attached. The second piece is the bag that catches the feces and clamps to the base. It seemed complicated and I was overwhelmed, but I was determined to read the learning material left for me. The nurse clamped the second piece while the base was attached to my skin. That hurt so bad. Why wouldn't you clamp it first and then attach it as one piece? She apologized for causing me more pain. Although I felt like she was sincere, I was just tired of hearing the word sorry from the staff. I accepted her apology and asked her not to ever do that again. She explained to me that there are also one-piece colostomy bags available and would use that one next time. I didn't understand, why not use it this time? I guess I couldn't say too much because this was my first time looking and engaging. It was at this time I realized I needed to be more vocal and active in this part of my treatment. It's important to voice your desires when it comes to your body because nobody is going to advocate for you better than you will for yourself.

After she left, I began reading the pamphlet and decided to call my besties because it was making me sad. I spoke to my besties Ali and Pri today. What I love about them is they never allow me to feel like I am going through anything. They spoke to me like I was at home. They told me the IV was feeding me Mac and Cheese, collard greens, ribs, curry chicken, cake and all the other foods that I love. We have been friends for over 20 years and I consider them sisters. They both live in South Florida and I told them not to come up to see me. The hospital was still under COVID restrictions. Due to the restrictions, I was only allowed one visitor per day. Although my mother and aunt were able to find ways around those rules, I didn't want my besties traveling and not be able to see me. Honestly, Ali doesn't like hospitals, so she was fine with the suggestion of not coming to see me while I was admitted. I promised to keep them updated as much as possible.

DAY 8: SURVIVING THE NIGHT SHIFT

It's Sunday morning and I was able to tune into my church online. My pastor was aware of what I was going through and prayed for me.

Let's talk about last night. At 11pm and 3am I had to call for urine clean up. Myles called the nurses' station to express his frustrations. After he called, the tech came rushing in as if the nurses' button wasn't pushed and I was told to wait. When a family member spends the night, the tech treats me really good. When I am there alone, the treatment is horrible. I have to wait 45 minutes for a response and the bed is soaked in urine because they think this little banana crap is better than coming to unhook the machine so I can go to the bathroom.

Cleaning the bed at 11pm, 3am, vitals, and medicine every three hours meant I got very little rest last night. The NG tube is still in place and my throat is extremely sore. The more I tried to speak, the more the tube was moving and essentially scratching my throat.

So here I am, NG tube, not able to bathe, painful to speak, no food, no liquids and soaked in urine at night. What type of care is this? Why do I deserve to be treated like this? I just want these bowels to wake up so I can get out of here. This is no way to treat a human being. Let me be clear, night shift tech, this is no way to treat anyone. My mom assured me that this will be all over soon.

I was able to walk six times around the nurses' station during the daytime. When I walk, I am being supported by the physical therapist or nurse with a strap. I used the IV stand to keep my balance. It has wheels so it's easy to push. I am not able to take the laps all at once because I am still experiencing shortness of breath and my steps are very short. It takes me 5 to10 minutes to do one lap.

After watching television for a while, the nurses let me get some rest. Normally, they encourage me to sit up in the chair and walk around. Today my body needed a break because last night I slept for approximately three hours total.

The tube in my nose was still putting out green bile. Although it wasn't a lot of output, it was still enough for the doctors to be concerned. The sound the tube made was disgusting. It felt like the sound was intensified during the night because it was quiet. The tube makes a loud, suctioning sound and I could see the bile leaving my nose and going into the "bucket" on the wall. The tape on my nose that was holding the tube in place started to come loose. This caused the tube to continuously shift. The more the tube moved, the more it hurt because it was rubbing the top of my nose. It became uncomfortable. The night nurse agreed to tighten the tube by adding more tape to hold the tube in place. The nurse put a lot of tape on it and it made me feel better. After tightening it with the tape, I noticed more bile starting to come from the tube. I guess I am going to have this tube in my nose longer than I anticipated.

My mom was home and she loves football. Her favorite team is the Steelers and they were playing tonight. We communicated through text and she was so happy. I watched the Steelers game with her and exchanged a series of text. I could just hear her yelling at the TV whenever they made a bad play. They played the Bengals and won by three. It was such a good game.

DAY 9: DEAR MOMMA

At 6am, the doctor's team came in for evaluation. She stuck a tube in my stoma and it was painful. The doctor is worried at this point because my bowels are still asleep. The doctor ordered more testing and scans. Before the team left, I advised them that I needed to be changed because I was laying in urine again. They said they would send someone in to get it changed. They also advised that they really didn't want me wearing that thing during the night. They wanted me up and walking to the bathroom.

After the team left, the tech came into my room. She advised that she gets off in five minutes and she's not changing me. I had to wait an additional hour for the dayshift to come into my room. When they came in, I told them what transpired, and they were furious. I provided the name of the tech and told them I never wanted to see her again.

After my mother dropped Marc off to school, she came to the hospital. I told her what happened, and she immediately stormed out of the room. Somebody was about to get it. I hadn't seen my mother this upset in a long time. She was always the one to be positive and tell me to be nice to the staff, no matter what is going on. When she got upset and left the room, I felt sorry for the tech who said that to me. Within thirty minutes, the head nurse was in my room asking me questions. I was given another apology! If I hear, I'm sorry one more time, I am going to lose it. Let's find a word to replace sorry with. That word sorry was working my last nerve.

My mother told them that they do not want to see the other side of her. I was scared for them and happy for me.

There was something different about my mother today. I asked her to tell me what was bothering her. She said nothing. I knew she wasn't telling the truth. I asked her again and she proceeded to tell me that she was frustrated.

The hospital still hadn't completed her FMLA paperwork for her job and her best friend/sister was gone back to South Florida. My mother's days now consisted of dropping my son to school, coming to the hospital, going home, making dinner and going to sleep. Her life has completely changed. She hasn't been back home, seen her friends, her beautician, co-workers or her sister. I understood her pain. She felt alone. My mother needed a support system too. I asked her if she expressed her feelings to my aunt and she said no. She didn't know how to tell her that she missed her without making her feel bad. My mother is the perfect example of what unconditional love is. Unexpectedly, her child almost died and because of it, she hasn't been to work in two weeks. She hasn't been back to south Florida for any reason. My mother has been at my house cooking, cleaning, and taking care of her grandchildren. She does this all with a smile on her face and love in her heart.

My mother made the ultimate sacrifice without any hesitation, and I thank God for her every day. When I make it out of this situation, I am going to do everything in my power to show her how much she is loved and appreciated. If it weren't for my mother, my entire family would be lost.

Dear Momma, I love you!!

She had to leave to pick up Marc from school and said she would come back. I really didn't want her to come back because it was too much driving. She told me that Marc really wanted to see me, and she said she would bring him to the hospital after school tomorrow. I was excited about that. My mom left for the day, and I tried to get some rest.

I had a very interesting conversation with Myles. He was working and I had to tell him what the tech did. He told me to do exactly what the doctor's team said, try to get up and go to the bathroom. I kept telling him that I would pee on the floor because the tubes were hooked to the machine. He said, oh well, you will just have to pee on the floor. It's better than laying in pee for hours because the night tech wants to be lazy. He told me he better not call again and hear that I was laying in urine. I just laughed and said okay. However, he was very serious. I could tell from the tone in his voice. It made sense, but I was still thinking about the person who would have to clean up the urine from the floor. It wouldn't be the selfish tech. It would be the cleaning staff. That wasn't fair to them. He assured me that it's not fair to anyone that the tech isn't doing their job and if I urinated on the floor, it was their fault and not mine.

Shortly afterwards, I was taken down for testing and it took all day. Contrast was put in through the tube. The purpose of the test was to see how things were flowing through my bowels. Hopefully, I hear good news tomorrow from my test results.

Tonight was my first night without that thing to catch my urine. I called for help to go to the bathroom and after 45 minutes of no help, I tried to make it to the bathroom by unhooking myself from the machine. It didn't work and I urinated on the floor while trying to make it to the bathroom. I wiped myself off and got back in the bed. Approximately fifteen minutes later, someone came into the room and I told them that the urine needed to be cleaned from the floor because I couldn't make it to the bathroom in time. The lady was not happy and said I needed to put that thing back on. I refused and told her if it takes 45 minutes to an hour to unhook someone from a machine, they were going to be cleaning up urine every four hours.

I don't understand why some people choose professions just to have a nasty attitude towards someone. I would have to say that Myles was correct. When I pushed the button to go to the bathroom after that, I had help within ten minutes. It's very sad that it took all of that to get the proper care that I deserved.

DAY 10: BRING ON THE TUBES

"Your bowels aren't waking up, would you consider going to rehab?", is what the doctor asked me. Lady, are you crazy? Absolutely not. You punctured my colon, you put me in this situation where I need a colostomy bag. I haven't been able to eat for over a week. I haven't taken a bath. My throat hurts because of the NG tube. I can barely walk without losing my breath. My mother hasn't been back home. I haven't been able to see my son or work and you want to send me to rehab because you can't figure out why my bowels aren't waking up? She must think I am a fool. There is no way I was letting anyone send me to rehab with a problem this serious. The test results revealed that it is taking my bowels six hours to do what a normal bowel does in one hour. Now, please explain to me how rehab was supposed to fix that problem? I have been very patient and quiet during this entire process, but she is really pushing it. I will remain right here until my body is functioning properly. I will not allow her to throw me away for a second time. This is a problem that she created, and I am staying right here until it is fixed. She could tell I was upset and started saying, "Oh no, I was just asking." Why did you think it was appropriate to ask me something like that? She had no answer for me and left my room.

My IV started leaking and needed to be replaced. I have lymphedema in my right arm, therefore IV's, blood draws, taking my blood pressure, etc.

are limited to my left arm. The nurse brought up a machine to find a vein to start another IV and they were unsuccessful. The machine highlights my veins and allows the nurse to stick the needle directly into it with minimal error. My arm was completely bruised. It looked like I had been in a terrible fight and lost.

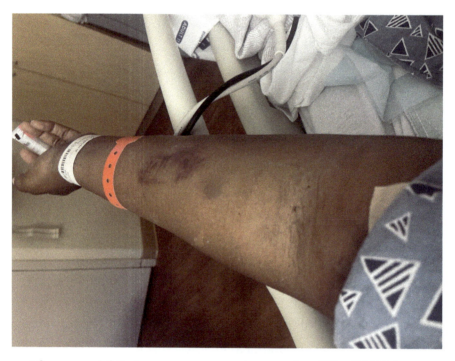

After several failed attempts at starting another IV, a PICC line was ordered to be placed on my left side. This order required me to be taken to another room because this is considered a small procedure. Before placing the PICC line, a sonogram was done in the area where the PICC line would be placed. The sonogram revealed a superficial blood clot under my left arm and I was advised that they would need to find another area to put the PICC line. Did you just say I had a blood clot? She said yes, but it's superficial and there is nothing to worry about. That made me worry even more. Nonetheless, the PICC line was inserted near my chest

DAY 10: BRING ON THE TUBES

area. The process wasn't painful and it was very quick. I had three little things hanging from my chest. I believe they are called CVC tubes. This PICC line will allow me to receive nutrients and the nurses can draw blood without any issues. This was excellent because every morning the nurses draw my blood and send it for testing. Although this PICC line is a great idea, all I keep thinking is, my poor little body is going through it.

By the time this procedure was done, it was the afternoon, and I was prepared to see my son. My mother called and it was the first time I heard her cry. She brought my son to the hospital to see me and security would not let him up because of COVID restrictions. You have got to be kidding me! All of this going on and I can't see my mom or my son today. It has been a total of nine days that I hadn't been able to see my son, hug him, or give him a kiss. I was looking forward to seeing him this afternoon and I feel like I failed him. I feel like I set him up to be sad and I took it hard. As a mother, we always try to make things better and the best thing I could do was FaceTime him. My son began asking questions and didn't understand why he couldn't see his mom. I could see the pain in his eyes and it disturbed me deeply. Although it was very painful to talk, I stayed on the phone with him for as long as he wanted. I answered every question he had and told him I love him so much. The million-dollar question was, mom when are you coming home? Still, I had no answers.

I sat in the chair for a long time today and took a trip around the nurses station five times. They were so proud of me. I felt like family with the day shift nurses and techs. Everyone knew who I was. Walking around the nurses' station became depressing. I said to myself, who would be depressed because they could walk? Me, I was depressed. Every time I walked out of my room, someone was being discharged. Someone was going home to be with their loved ones. I wasn't going anywhere but in circles. I was going back to my room in the corner and wait for my bowels to "wake up".

I had no visitors this afternoon and I was struggling to find something to watch on television. I asked my mother to bring my computer tomorrow so I could watch different TV shows from the apps that I downloaded. She knew I wasn't able to talk for long, so she sent me this text: "Love you and we are going to beat this. With the help of the Lord, everything is possible."

The nurse comes in with this huge brown bag that smelled very sweet. I said, oh goodness what are we doing now? She said it is your breakfast, lunch, and dinner. I just laughed because what else could you describe it as. I said at least it smells good. Hook me up. She hooked up the bag to the machine and my body was getting "food" through the PICC line. Although my body was getting what it needed, I was so hungry and thirsty.

DAY 11: WHAT LAWSUIT?

The drainage tube from my stomach was removed today. With the tube being removed from my stomach, I am left with the NG-tube in my nose, PICC line in my chest with three tubes hanging, and the colostomy bag. Although the drainage tube was removed, my stomach was hurting so I requested a heating pad. The heating pad provided some relief. They didn't know why my stomach was hurting, but I believe it was from the pain medicine I was receiving through the PCA machine. I noticed every time I would push the button for pain medicine to be administered, my stomach would cramp for a few minutes and then the cramps would subside. I decided to tell the nurses what I was experiencing and that I believed it was coming from the pain medicine that I was getting from the PCA. The plan was to tell the doctor and find out their recommendation.

As I was taking my slow stroll around the nurses' station, I was advised that I needed to go for another CT scan. I already knew the scan was going to show that there was no bowel movement because nothing had changed since the last time and there was no output from my stoma.

I told my mom not to come visit me today because all I was doing was crying. I didn't want her to see me this way.

My mom agreed to come tomorrow and check on the status of her FMLA paperwork that she submitted to the hospital for her job. My mother was trying to save her job and help me save my life at the same time.

I felt so bad that she was going through this. This wasn't fair to her at all. She didn't deserve any of this. My mother has her moments of sadness and there is nothing wrong with that. I have my moments and will continue to have them because I am a human being. I just try not to stay in those bad moments too long because being depressed is no fun and it's not how God intends me to be.

As I laid in the bed on my back, I started researching colostomy bags, how to take care of them, support groups for black women with colostomy bags and stores for supplies. The real surprise was, there isn't a colostomy supply store that you can visit in person. Everything related to the colostomy bags must be ordered online. This is going to be more difficult than I imagined.

There was a lot of information online as it related to the colostomy bag. I found sites that had bag covers. I even found support groups on social media that I joined. I followed one black woman on social media that was very open about her colostomy bag experience. It gave me hope.

The major difference between myself and the other women I encountered online is they have chronic illnesses associated with their colostomy bag. I didn't have an illness, only the mistake of a doctor.

After describing the incident to my newly found online support group, everyone said, I know you are going to sue them. I was like, "I am working on it". The truth is, no lawyer would take my case. These are excuses that my mom was given from these attorneys about why they couldn't take my case: I didn't die, there was no permanent damage, I am expected to recover, and I can't sue that hospital. I couldn't believe what my mom was hearing from different attorneys. Thank God I didn't die. Nobody would've known what the doctor did during my hysterectomy because she failed to report it and I am sure she wasn't going to say anything if I passed away. They probably would've attributed my death to complications from surgery.

Let's talk about permanent damage. I had a healthy colon that was punctured. Who's to say that the lifespan of my colon hasn't been shortened because of this? Who's to say that I won't experience complications in the future due to this puncture? I also would like to know who limited permanent damage to internal organs or a physical disability? What about the damage to my mental health? I can't even begin to describe the emotional and mental instability that I experience several times throughout the day. This isn't normal and I wasn't this way before she messed with my colon.

Does anyone care about that? Does anyone care about my mother possibly losing her job to help me? Does anyone care about me losing clients, losing money, losing my mind? What about my children's mental stability? There is no compensation for that.

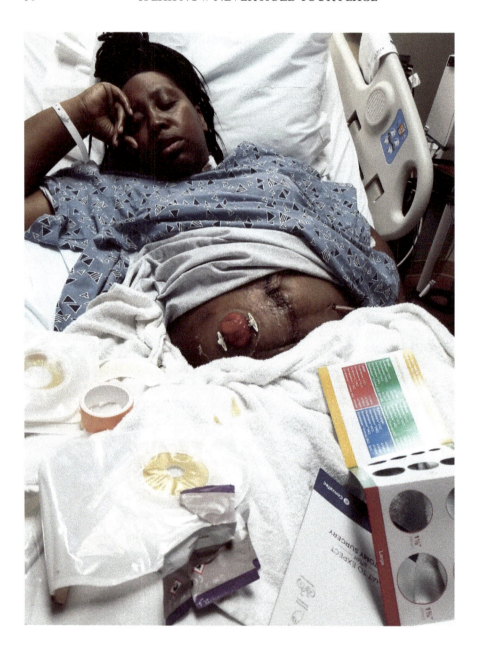

The excuse that I am going to recover is ridiculous. I didn't know that being resilient meant that you shouldn't be compensated when people cause you damage. The bottom line is this, if the lawyers aren't going to make a bunch of money, they tell you that you don't have a case. I have the feeling that nobody really cares about the black woman that almost died. I wonder what would've happened if I was famous, related to another doctor, or an attorney. Would their position change? I may never know the answer to that question.

DAY 12: SURPRISE

The nurse comes in with this small needle that I have never seen before. I asked her, "What is that for?" She said she would explain to me shortly. After she was done making her notes in the computer, she turned to me and said your sugar levels are high and the doctor has ordered insulin shots. Seriously? What did y'all give me to make my sugar levels high? No answer. Just a confused look. Imagine how confused I am in this very moment. The nurse stated that they needed to prick my finger and a small amount of blood went into a hand-held machine. That machine gave a number that was an indicator of my sugar levels. If that number was too high, I would be getting an insulin shot in my thigh. Goodness people. I don't think my body has any additional space for needles to be poked into it. I feel like I keep waking up to news that has nothing to do with me getting out of here. Now I have high sugar levels and need insulin. They do not suspect it will last forever, but for now, this is life. Insulin shots.

Another nurse came in and changed the colostomy bag again today. This time I made sure the clamp was already attached before pressing on my stomach. The lady was excited because the stoma was pink and looked healthy. I honestly didn't care to see it or know about it. I just wanted her to change it and leave. She was extremely nice, but I just found out my sugar levels are high, I need insulin shots in my leg, and I still can't eat or drink anything by mouth. This has not been a good day at all.

In walked more nurses with more news from the doctor. It was recommended that a G-tube be placed in my stomach since I hadn't been able to eat or drink for such a long period of time. I agreed with this and down I went for another procedure. The placement of the G-tube was successful, and I was over it for the day.

This procedure would eventually allow the NG-tube from my nose to be removed. Once that tube is removed, I would be able to have clear liquids by mouth. I understood and I was ready to embark on another journey. This hospital stay was full of surprises and never-ending journeys.

My mother decided to come late today. Usually when she comes this late, she will stay overnight with me, so I was happy. She gave me the computer, but I didn't watch anything. We just talked about life and enjoyed each other's company. She helped me to the bathroom, unhooked my machines, and I had no accidents. The nurse had come to give me another insulin shot and I was over it. I didn't want to see anymore nurses for the evening.

I heard another knock at the door and I immediately closed my eyes. I told my mom to tell them I was asleep. I didn't feel like talking or answering any questions. My mom didn't listen to anything I said. She touched my arm and said, "Eboni, the nurse is here to see you." Now I know she just heard me tell her that I didn't want to see anyone. That didn't matter to her. She said, "Eboni, open your eyes because the nurse is here to talk to you." I really didn't care who was there. I wasn't getting ready to open my eyes. She said it again, so against my better judgment, I opened my eyes.

Myles was standing at the foot of my bed smiling! I was so happy to see him that I could've jumped out of the bed. I said, "What are you doing here?" My mom was looking at me smiling and he gave me a hug. He said he got the call that I wasn't doing good and he had to come see me and get me back on track. I just laughed at him because he was so serious. Luckily for the hospital, they switched the night techs to someone that was more helpful. Myles had a few choice words ready for that person who refused to change me, but I never saw that tech again. My mom said, "Okay, I am going home to get some rest. You got your protector here now." We laughed and she gave me a hug before going home.

Myles began sharing with me the prayers his mom/our mom sent, along with the thoughtful words and well wishes from his other family members, friends and co-workers. That made me feel good and embarrassed at the same time. I wonder how many people know that I have a colostomy bag? The answer was everybody. Myles needed support and it wasn't my place to tell him who he should receive it from. Myles told me that his aunt, who is a retired ICU nurse, advised him that I should be chewing bubble gum to help wake up my bowels. She said chewing gum would stimulate the bile in my body. He gave me some gum. I wasn't approved to be chewing this by the doctor, but I put it in my mouth and began chewing anyway. I then asked him to sneak me some of my favorite soda. He said no. I was thinking, dude this is part of the reason you are here; to make sure I am okay and sneak me some food and soda. He told me that I tried it and he would not give me any food or soda. He ate his sub in front of me, drank his soda, and it looked so good. I was so jealous and hungry. I was secretly hoping the sub would fall on the floor or something, just so I could say, that's what you get. It didn't fall and I really admired the fact that he came all the way up here, in his work clothes, just to make sure I was truly okay. After he ate, he took a shower in the bathroom in my room. That shower sounded so good. It sounded like rain drops falling. I hadn't heard the sound of a shower in twelve days. I was able to brush my teeth daily and wipe down, but no shower. After he got out of the shower, he asked me to find something good on TV to watch. That was a joke. The TV stations play the same shows all night long. We used that time to talk until my pain medicine kicked in. He held my hand until I fell asleep.

Beep, beep, beep, beep was the sound that woke him up continuously throughout the night. For some reason, the machines kept saying there was air in my line that was attached to the big brown nutrients bag. After the fifth time of this going off, Myles learned how to make it stop on his own. In between the beeping sounds, my vitals were taken every three hours and I received insulin shots in between my vitals. Myles asked if they could all come in at one time to do what needed to be done so I could rest. That would be the logical thing to do, but they never did this. I was happy he got to experience what I really go through during the night. It made him admire my strength even more because he felt like what was happening at night didn't make any logical sense. I agreed with him, but this is day twelve and I am used to it by now.

We both fell asleep, but within two hours, it was time to get up again.

DAY 13: PARTY TIME

It was 6am when the doctors team comes in, wakes me up, and asks, "How are you feeling?" I said, "I don't know, I just woke up". Myles laughed at me and said, "What kind of answer is that?" I personally didn't see anything wrong with it because they woke me up. I don't know how I feel yet, my brain hasn't processed it. He couldn't believe I said that and kept laughing. The doctors advised that the tube from my nose would be removed. Thank goodness. I have been waiting for this day since it was put back in. I was excited to have the tube from my nose removed. My throat was extremely sore, and my voice was cracking. For the past eight days, each time I tried to talk, the tube felt like it was scratching my throat, which essentially made it feel like it was "raw". After the tube was removed, I was placed on a clear, liquid diet. And guess what? I was told to chew bubble gum. Whoo hooo!!! I ordered cranberry juice, apple juice, broth, Gatorade and orange flavored chewing gum. I was like a kid in a candy store. I haven't been this happy since I've been in the hospital. The tube being removed from my nose made me feel like I was becoming myself again. The top of my nose started hurting so bad. Myles took pictures of the top of my nose, and it had a huge scab inside of it. I wanted to scratch it so bad, but decided against it.

Also, now that the tube was out, I could begin taking morphine and oxycodone by mouth. The pain medicine that I was taking via the PCA was discontinued. I was curious to see how this new regimen of pain medicine by mouth would work.

It was Friday and Myles called his job and advised them that he wasn't coming into work today. It's official. This man really loves me because he never misses work. I mean, he goes into work even when he doesn't have to. I said, "You called into work for little 'ole me" and all he could do was smile.

The nurse came in and checked my sugar levels. It was high and I had to get another insulin shot in my leg. Myles suggested that I alternate the shots in my leg because my left thigh was bruised. I didn't want two bruised legs, so I decided against alternating the shots in my legs. One bruised leg was enough for me.

Myles wanted to see my chart so he could converse with his aunt about what was going on with me. He likes to know everything, and I always tell him that he's just nosy. I logged into my medical records through my online patient portal, and he began reading certain things to his aunt. She explained the medicine, tubes, and the colostomy bag to me in a way that made sense. Myles forced me to deal with what I was going through in reference to the colostomy bag. He made me look at it, read about it, take pictures of it, and he tried to name it. Okay, hold up now. We are not naming this thing. You are taking it too far sir. The literature said that the stoma has no feeling and he tested that theory out by pushing it while my eyes were closed. I didn't feel anything. The literature was correct, the stoma has no feeling. It is the skin around the stoma that has feeling.

It was time to take a walk around the nurses' station. Myles and the tech assisted me. I was not able to walk alone because I was still considered a fall risk. I didn't feel comfortable walking alone, so I was happy to have the help. Myles was walking too fast, and I told him to slow down. Sir, where are we going? Why are we walking so fast? The look he gave me implied that I may have hurt his feelings. After the two seconds stare down, I kept moving at my own pace. After we made a few more rounds, I was ready to go back to the room. As we got to the door, I told him that we couldn't go through at the same time. He looked at me, laughed, and said, "I know." It was so funny because I said it just to get on his nerves.

The medicine started kicking in and I wanted to get some rest. While I got some rest, Myles left and got some fast food. I tried to convince him to get the hospital food because it's really good, but he decided not to. I think he just wanted some fresh air.

While I was asleep, the alert for my ring camera kept going off. I looked at it and to my surprise, some of my family members were at the house. I almost cried because these particular family members showed up and they don't just go out of town for nothing. Your girl is feeling really special right now!

My mom texted me and said "the gang is here". I was so happy because this family member makes us all laugh, tells it likes it is, and loves us so much. She will curse you out in a minute, but it comes from a place of love. I told my mom to enjoy the family and I couldn't wait to see them tomorrow. Being that only one person was allowed into the hospital room, we developed a plan to sneak them up. I hope it works tomorrow because I really wanted to see everyone that came up.

When Myles came back with his food, I told him who was in town. He said, "They are going to have a good time at the house this weekend." I gave him the phone to show him the video from the ring camera.

He needed my password to open it. Without thinking about it, I gave it to him. Oh boy, I must be in love too. I just gave this man the password to my phone. There is nothing in it for me to be concerned about, but it's just the idea that Myles has the password to my phone. He better look at that video and give the phone right back is what I was thinking. Don't go looking at any pictures, text messages, emails; none of that. He gave the phone back as soon as he finished looking at the video.

Later in the evening, my daughter walked into the room with my other family members. "Awwwwwwww! How did you get up here? Why weren't you on the ring camera?" I was so happy that my daughter surprised me. They had flowers and big balloons. I was so happy! Myles left to get food after they arrived. These were the visitors that I didn't know I needed. We laughed, took pictures, and made videos. We just had a good time. The nurses didn't kick them out and I can't reveal how we snuck them in. It was getting late and they left.

Myles came back with his food and the smell was making me nauseous. I asked him to leave the room and eat the food. He did not like that and said it was the same exact food from yesterday. I don't know why I was feeling this way, but that food had to go. Myles said if he wasn't so far away from home, he would've gone back immediately. I couldn't tell if he was joking or not, but I did feel bad after he left. I didn't want to hurt his feelings, but I didn't want to throw up either. He left the room to eat his food, then came back. Of course when he came back into the room, he talked about the food situation for about twenty minutes. He said he thought I was joking, but when he realized that I was serious, it made absolutely no sense because it was the same food. I just laughed and told him, I don't know what the reason was, but I was nauseous and I was not trying to vomit. He understood. Or so I thought.

While Myles was gone, I called my mother and told her what happened. She said we would be okay and not to think too deep into it. I asked her how things were going at the house. She said they were cooking, watching TV, and having a good time. My mother hasn't sounded this happy since I've been in this hospital. Mom deserved this.

DAY 13: PARTY TIME

This weekend was going to be good for her. Mom was finally getting a break from this place.

DAY 14: MOTHER/DAUGHTER BOND

Today I learned how to vent the G-tube. I was under the impression that if I was feeling nauseous, and had to vent the G-tube often, the NG-tube would be going back into my nose. You know I was not going to tell them if I was feeling nauseous. I did not want that tube back down my nose again. I enjoyed my clear liquids, being able to talk, and my throat was starting to feel better. Whenever the doctor asked me if I was feeling nauseous, the answer was no. It was the truth, and I was happy about that.

The nurses came into my room and kept stating that it was "toasty", meaning they were hot. The hospital rooms allow you to control the temperature with the thermostat on the wall. I didn't think it was hot. I looked over at Myles and he said, "Yes, it's hot in here." "Really, why didn't you say anything?" He said, "You're the patient and it's your room." I couldn't believe everyone was hot and I was cold. I had so many blankets on my bed and I was still cold. The techs came into the room and I asked them if it was hot in my room. They said yes. I just laughed because I was literally freezing and everyone else was hot. Nobody told me that I had it like a boiler room. I turned the air down for them to cool them off and just asked for more heating blankets.

My family members came back to visit me today. The first thing Myles does is tell them that I kicked him out the room with his food. They were on my side and told him that they would've kicked him out too. They asked him how could eat in front of me knowing I had the tube in my nose? I was like, "Yeah get him." He kept trying to plead his case and it didn't work. He finally gave up. You aren't going to win in a room full of women.

Myles went to the house to take a bath, get some rest, and give me time with the girls.

My daughter laid in the bed with me, and it felt really good. We had to be careful because of the bag and all the other tubes, but we made it work. We haven't laid in the same bed since she was a child. We had a very intimate conversation that I will keep between us. I will just say that our bond became stronger, and I am grateful for this.

I asked the girls if they wanted to see the bag and they said no. I was so happy they said no because I really didn't want them to see it either.

The nurses came into my room and they told me I was having a party in my room! Oh yes, it was definitely a party. My family ordered the hospital food and couldn't believe how good it was. I took six laps around the nurses' station and they were cheering me on like I was walking on a fashion runway. I just loved their energy and having them with me in the hospital. We took pictures, made videos, and eventually the fun had to end. They went back to my home and I was left alone for approximately two hours.

In those two hours, I got some sleep. The door opened and in walks my mom. I told her to stay away for the weekend, but she wasn't going to do that. Nobody listens to me anymore and its okay. She said that she needed to come check on me and see this G-tube in my stomach. She was so happy to see me without the tube in my nose. She then proceeded to tell me that I looked good. I didn't feel pretty, but I was appreciative of the nice words. You're my mom, you're supposed to say I'm pretty. She laughed at me and said that she was happy that I was in good spirits. She stayed with me until Myles came back.

As happy as I was throughout the day, it is the nighttime that overwhelms me. During the night, it's quiet and there isn't a lot of activity.

It's just me, with my thoughts. The realization started to set in that my bowels were not functioning like they should. I began to become depressed. I just laid with my eyes closed and told Myles, "I'm tired". A few moments later, gospel music filled the room. I lifted my hands to give praise and he said, "We aren't going to talk like that. You are strong, you are a fighter, and God got us." I opened my eyes he grabbed my hand, and said, "We aren't doing that. You keep fighting okay. I don't ever want to hear you say, "I'm tired". I said okay. He began to rub my feet and then said, "My entire hand can fit around your ankles, look". What kind of statement is that? He was excited and I was thinking, how skinny am I? How much weight did I lose? He was trying to uplift me; However, making me notice that my legs were that small was not uplifting at all. Poor Myles couldn't catch a break with me. I told him to just put the Jesus music back on and leave my ankles alone. I didn't even want a foot rub anymore. We laughed at each other because that's what we do!

Myles got hungry and asked for permission to eat food. Really Myles? That's what we are doing? Eat your food and stop playing. He reminded me that I kicked him out the other day and he didn't want to get kicked out again today. I just rolled my eyes and said, "Well starve." He laughed at me. I think he says stuff just to hear me say something to make him laugh. He got food, ate it in the room, and there were no issues.

While I was laying in bed, I started paying attention to my legs, my arms, and my stomach. I was extremely skinny. I looked at my pictures and my face was very narrow. I hope I don't look sick. I hope when I get out of here, people don't look at me like "what happened to her"? I wasn't opposed to losing weight, but not like this. I look sick, have a colostomy bag, and a G-tube. Myles told me that I was beautiful and none of that stuff mattered. Inside I was like you are supposed to say that, even if it's not true. I accepted the compliments because I know he was trying to cheer me up. I prayed that he really meant what he said.

Today was eventful and I couldn't wait to go to sleep. Throughout the night, I experienced hot flashes. It was weird because up until this point, I was always cold. My nurse gave me a fan that clipped to my bed and it cooled me down.

DAY 15: SELF EDUCATION

Last night was good. I only vented the G-Tube once. I didn't have any urine accidents and overall, I felt better.

Today it was time for everyone to go back home. Reality started to sink in and I was sad. I got to see everyone for the last time before they traveled back to South Florida. They gave me hugs, kisses, and we took more pictures before they left. The room was filled with flowers and I felt very special.

As I was laying down in the bed, I noticed the sheet around my stomach area was wet. I was so scared and thought the bag was leaking. I removed the sheet and there was fluid coming from my belly button. Oh my goodness, what in the world is going on now. Do I ring this button for help? Do I just lay here and not say anything? I can't take any more bad news. Maybe I did too much this weekend with my family members and Myles. I just laid there for a while and pretended the fluid leakage didn't exist. The leakage didn't stop so I had to press the button and tell the nurses what was happening. They notified the doctors and told me not to worry. The fluid was clear and did not have a smell, so I was feeling okay about it.

It was determined that the fluid was from the incision site and my health was not in danger. The fluid would eventually stop and there was nothing for me to do but take it easy.

Today I drank a chocolate milkshake and it taste so good. I don't know if a different person made it in the cafeteria, but it was extra good today.

After everyone left, I got on my computer and researched the side effects of having a hysterectomy. I have been so consumed with my colon being punctured that I haven't even learned anything about my hysterectomy. I just assumed the hysterectomy went well. We haven't spoken about that procedure since I have been in the hospital. It was up to me to educate myself. The side effects of a hysterectomy included hot flashes, night sweats, and mood swings. This explained why I was feeling extremely hot and sweaty last night. Hot flashes are no fun and unpredictable. Without warning, my body gets extremely hot and sweat starts pouring. It feels like someone poured warm water all over my body. I don't think I have had any mood swings as of yet. Knowing that I could have mood swings gives me the advantage of controlling them. I am going to make it a priority to be aware of my feelings and not use the hysterectomy as an excuse to have mood swings. I'm going to try and be extremely nice to people.

After that, I did more research on the colostomy bag. I didn't know what it would be like when my bowels woke up. What was supposed to happen? I have asked the team of doctors and they just told me that I would know. That was not helpful at all. How would I know? I never had a colostomy bag and it just didn't make any sense. My research revealed that the bag would fill with air and that is how I would know. It would be like a fart in the bag.

Basically, I needed to fart to live.

DAY 16: LET IT OUT

The doctors team came in early this morning and pushed on my stomach. It hurt so bad that I put the heating pad on it to ease the pain. My body was tolerating the oral pain medicine regimen very well. I wasn't feeling nauseous, my pain level remained below 5, and I did three laps. I was walking, sitting in the chair for longer periods of time, chewing gum, and guess what happened? The colostomy bag started leaking. I bet you thought I was going to say I farted.

The nurse team changed the bag and my skin around the stoma was very red and sensitive to the touch. How do you cure that? I was so confused. The bag is attached to me 24/7 and there is no time to let my skin "breathe" so it can heal. Just another obstacle and side effect of having this bag. I opted for a one-piece colostomy bag because I felt like it would be easier for me to handle once I left the hospital.

My sugar levels were high, and I had to get another insulin shot in my leg. When will this end? As I laid in the bed, I had another hot flash. Thank goodness I had the fan clipped to my bed. It felt like a miniature air conditioner blowing on me. It felt so good.

My mom arrived and we talked about how good the weekend was. I did three laps with my mom and I had to use the bathroom. When I got to the bathroom, I screamed for my mom. She came running in, not knowing what to expect. I said mom, I farted!! The bag was full of air and I thought it was going to burst. She got her phone and took pictures. Who knew that farting would be so exciting! After taking pictures, my mom called the nurses and they came in jumping for joy. They told me to wait for the doctor to come in and see it. She was there in two minutes. She was so happy.

My mood immediately changed when the doctor asked, "Do you want to go home today?" Oh my goodness, lady!! Why do you keep trying to send me home? I only farted once, relax. I told her it's too soon. Shouldn't I be evaluated for at least 24 hours? Shouldn't I learn how to empty the bag properly? Can I take a shower now? I respectfully told her that it was not time to go home. It was time for me to be monitored and tomorrow, if I felt comfortable, I would go home.

She agreed and left the bathroom. I learned how to empty the bag and close it with the help of the nurse. I was told that while I was at home, I would need to measure the output and write it down. If there was too much output, it means that I was dehydrated and that was not good. I had to remember not to eat foods such as corn, peanuts, salads, popcorn, pizza, raw fruits, and spicy and greasy food; just to name a few.

The nurse came in and went over my discharge instructions. They were confident that I would be going home tomorrow morning. They also told me that they would coordinate for me to have a home health aide nurse to help with the care of the colostomy bag. That made me feel like I would not be alone and have help while at home, adjusting to my new normal.

I could finally take a shower. I didn't want the nurses to give me a shower, but I couldn't do it alone because I was still considered a fall risk. My mother agreed to supervise my shower. While in the shower, all I did was cry. I was crying because I didn't have the energy to bathe myself. How did this happen? I was walking around the hospital nurses station daily, sitting in the chair, but still had no energy to bathe myself. I felt so helpless. My mom allowed me to cry and told me it would be alright. She finished giving me a shower and I felt ashamed, but clean.

Shortly after my shower, my mother left the hospital to go shopping for food and other items in preparation for me to come home.

I called Myles to give him the update. He was excited and agreed that I should stay to be evaluated. He wanted me to stay longer than one more day. However, I felt good about only staying for an additional 24 hours and then going home. We had a difference of opinion of how long I should remain in the hospital, but we didn't let that overshadow the good news. Your girl was farting in the bag, and it felt so good.

The massage therapist came in and I couldn't have been more excited. One more massage before I went home was appreciated.

That happiness was short lived. My mom texted me that the cable and internet was disconnected. While I was fighting to stay alive, the bills were piling up. I forgot all about the bills. My son needs the internet to do his homework. The internet is a necessity in my home. My mother paid the bill to have it reconnected and I was extremely grateful. My mother felt bad that the cable was disconnected, and I told her that it wasn't her fault. At no time did paying bills cross my mind while I was in this hospital. I felt like I was being selfish by not thinking about the bills. My mom told me not to feel bad and concentrate on getting better. She advised me that she didn't see the cable bill and that's why she didn't pay it. I am so blessed to have her as my mother. The cable bill is paperless and that's why she didn't know it was past due. I asked her was she able to figure out how to pay it? She said the number was on the television and she took care of it. I promised to pay her back every penny and she said that she would not take any money from me. She said that she would see me in the morning. I told her not to tell Marc that I was coming home because I wanted to surprise him.

The night crew was excited to know that I passed gas, my bowels were awake, and I would be going home tomorrow. Tonight was a good night.

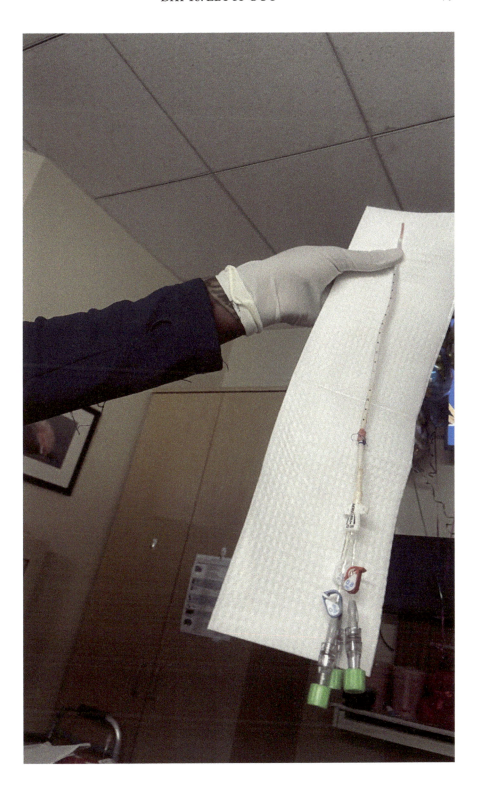

DAY 17: TIME TO LIVE

DAY 17: TIME TO LIVE

I had my final visit from the doctor's team this morning at 6am. The orders to be discharged were confirmed.

My mother arrived and we were almost ready to leave. She asked me how my night went, and I told her that it went very well.

The nurse came into my room with orders to remove The PICC line. The PICC line was removed, and my mother took pictures of it. We couldn't believe how long the tube was. Wow is all that I could think to myself. My mother had my clothes and shoes for me to change into. I took one more shower and changed into my clothes that I would be leaving the hospital in. I emptied the colostomy bag without help from the nurse and they assured me that I did it correctly. I was proud of myself for being able to empty the bag without making a mess.

The nurses gave my mother a cart to place my flowers, balloons, and other materials on. The cart made it easier for her to get all these things to the car. I gave my nurses and the techs a hug because they were always nice to me.

It was time to say goodbye to the hospital. Someone from the transport department arrived with a wheelchair. I got in the wheelchair and my mother was right behind me with a cart full of items. We got into the elevator and headed to the first floor. As the elevator was going down, I was thinking about how I was going to make everyone proud of me by continuing to be strong, listen to my body, advocate for myself, and give God all the glory for what He has brought me through. As I was wheeled down the hallway and saw the doors open, tears filled my eyes as the sun hit my face. The car pulls up and the time has come for me to embark on this new journey with a colostomy bag. It was time to live.

ACKNOWLEDGEMENTS

Special Thank You to the following:

My mother, Linda. There aren't enough words to express my love and gratitude for you. You are the best mother and I am blessed that you are mine.

My children Bri and Marc for supporting and believing in this book. I am so proud of both of you and honored to be your mother.

My niece, Ash for listening to all of my ideas, crying with me and all the sacrifices you made during this journey. I appreciate you and I am so proud of you.

My nephew, Tray for constantly calling, checking on me, making me laugh and traveling to spend time with me.

My aunt Caron for loving me, taking care of me, supporting me and making me laugh through some of the pain.

My pastor and church family at Revealing Truth for your continuous prayers and support.

All of my cousins for keeping me uplifted in prayer and laughing in the group chats.

My big sis and big bro for the weekly check-ins, unconditional support and prayers.

My bonus mom and aunt for the daily prayers, laughs and medical knowledge.

ACKNOWLEDGEMENTS

My best friend Ali, since I was six years old for loving me like a sister, praying, and inspiring me everyday.

My best friend Pri, since high school for loving me, praying and encouraging me every step of the way.

My best friend Meshia, for visiting me in the hospital, making sure my braids always look good and supporting me.

My friend Chele, who traveled from up north to be with me, listens to my crazy stories and gives the best advice.

Godsister and nieces, for making me laugh, visiting, bringing balloons, and being a support system for my kids.

Sorority sisters Mel and Tan. Along with their extended family for the flowers, phone calls and prayer pillow.

Mommination for being the village that I need, the zoom calls, prayers and love.

To my realtor friends of Allure Realty who sent flowers, food, prayers and encouraging words.

Editor, Latrice Scott for the honest feedback and edits.

Photographer, Erick Robinson for the amazing book cover photo.

Makeup Artist, Cherry aka "Makeupmadnessbycherry" for making me feel beautiful each time you do my makeup.

Videographers Delvin Peterson and "Chuck" for capturing the visuals of this project.

Last but not least,

My significant other, your prayers, love and support continues to be the cure to many things. Thank you for listening and saving my life. This would've been a different outcome, had it not been for you. I love you.

ABOUT THE AUTHOR

Eboni Stiff was born and raised in the inner city of Miami, Florida. Eboni earned her High School Diploma from Miami Northwestern Senior High in the early 2000's. Eboni believed that the only way to escape the inner city was through college. Immediately after high school, she moved to Tampa, Florida where she attended college. She earned a Bachelors of Social Work from the University of South Florida. After working as a social worker for a few years, Eboni returned to Miami, Florida to earn her Masters of Social Work from Barry University.

While it has always been a dream of hers to help others ,life positioned Eboni where she would be the one in need of help. From her twenties until the present day, Eboni has survived 19 surgeries, scoliosis, glaucoma, became a mother of two, unemployed and a breast cancer patient.

It was her faith, resiliency and support from her family, pastor and friends that turned her tests into testimonies. She continues to be a great mother, breast cancer survivor and a serial entrepreneur.

Eboni became an author to be an inspiration to others by sharing her life's journey with the world.

Milton Keynes UK
Ingram Content Group UK Ltd.
UKHW020640100124
435787UK00007B/25